D1248876

St. Louis Community College

Library

5801 Wilson Avenue
St. Louis, Missouri 63110

 PRINTED IN U.S.A.

23-263-002

Statues of the Grass

STATUES OF THE GRASS

James Applewhite

The University of Georgia Press, Athens

Library of Congress Catalog Card Number: 74-21904
International Standard Book Number: 0-8203-0372-0
The University of Georgia Press, Athens 30602
© 1975 by the University of Georgia Press
Printed in the United States of America

To the Memory of William Blackburn

Acknowledgments

The author and the publisher gratefully acknowledge permission to reprint these poems which originally appeared in the publications here noted: "Driving through a Country that Is Vanishing," *Esquire;* "Jogging on the New Construction," "Poets, Now," "The Man," "Bordering Manuscript," and "Revisitings," *Poetry;* "William Blackburn, Riding Westward," "The Sunplane," and "State Road 134," *Sewanee Review;* "Leaf Mirrors," *The Young American Poets* (Chicago, 1968); "Gift of Inheritance," *Crazy Horse;* "War Summer," *New American Review;* "Combat Station" and "Zeppelin Fantasy," *Virginia Quarterly Review;* "Visit with Artina," *Michigan Quarterly Review;* "The Homeplace" (published as "Last Crop"), *Mill Mountain Review;* "On the Homefront" and "A Vigil," *Southern Poetry Review;* "Cartographers" (published as "An Episode of War"), *Granite;* "A Kid at the County Fair," "Discardings," and "A Southern Elegy," *American Poetry Review;* "My Grandfather's Funeral," *Shenandoah;* "Eden's Dinosaur," *Greensboro Review;* "At Raleigh Memorial Gardens," *The Back Door.*

Contents

I

Driving through a Country that Is Vanishing   3
Jogging on the New Construction   4
State Road 134   5
My Grandfather's Funeral   7

II

Poets, Now   11
The Sunplane   12
Leaf Mirrors   13
William Blackburn, Riding Westward   14

III

Looking for a Home in the South   19
Discardings   21
Visit with Artina   22
Bordering Manuscript   24

IV

To Alexander Solzhenitsyn, In Exile   27
A Kid at the County Fair   28
The Homeplace   29
Revisitings   33

V

Zeppelin Fantasy   37
War Summer   38
Cartographers   39
At Raleigh Memorial Gardens   41

VI

Eden's Dinosaur   45
The Man   47
A Southern Elegy   49
Visiting Chancellorsville   51

VII
Gift of Inheritance: A Sequence

The Capsized Boat   55
Lawn and Light   56
On the Homefront   57
A Vigil   58
A Garden's Season   59
Iron River   60
With Darkening Foliage   61
Diamond of Shadow   62
A Forge of Words   63
Combat Station   64
To Forgive this Inheritance   65
Images, Burning   66
The Dragon's Teeth   67
Infant Hero   68
Stones of a Boundary   69

I

Driving through a Country that Is Vanishing

It begins to snow in a country
Between the past and what I see,
Soft flakes like eyelids softly descending,
Closing about branches, orchards of pecans,
Like washpot soot streaked in lines on the sky

Or is it that these husks empty of nuts
Are moving upward among the flakes they have suspended,
Like eyesockets gaping or a mockery of birds

So that a girl by the name of Mary Alice Taylor
Sings across this air from the seventh grade.
"Billie he come to see me. Billie he come
Last night." A mole, color of clear skin,
Swims by her nose. Flakes condense the light.

"Billie he asked me to be his wife, 'course I said alright."

Snow as if holding the country houses
Apart to be inspected, unsilvered
Mirror that lets float out of its depths
As from an old ocean of no dimension
Unlimited objects, leather tack and
Spokes of surreys, china
Long broken, whittled horses
Everything their hands would have touched.

Jogging on the New Construction

I run for my heart. An earthmover
Trundles at two hundred yards, its mantis speed unreal,
Like the dream-jumps of African antelopes.
The tracks of these animals are knotted and palpable
(Will they one day be fossilized in shale?):
Print of the Great American Earthmover, *terra omnivorous;*
Whole herds of hoofprints of the Sheepfoot Roller, *packederma
epidemia.*

I follow what seems an alligator's hide in clay:
The armored tread of the Bulldozer *bellicosus,*
Enemy of earth. Cloud rubs over like the weather's last
Cumulus. Trees stand skittish at the stream.

State Road 134

Down N.C. 134 past the township of Troy:
places not much in anyone's thoughts,
Wadesboro, Mt. Gilead, Calvary Church.
One yard spired
with the heartening thumb-bells of foxglove.
Road going past where the quick dog evaded
a truck in the monstrous heat: where
a hawk lay dead in a rumple of feathers,
a cow stood still under sweet gum scrub
and switched its tail.

I witnessed the chimney of a house long burnt
beside a ditchbank flooded with Cherokee rose.

And a field at my random turning
laid open and alone,
sky's rim back like an eyelid fringed
with the clay soil's fledgling pines.
Two board shacks with
windowpanes crushed by the heat,
paint bruised off by their weight of deprivation.

What balm of Gilead
descends for this mother, baby
on the hip of her luminous jeans?
In what hollow of mind
has even Christ held such features?

Face of a black boy vacant almost
as the country turning,
fields' loneliness sitting on his eyelids
too pure almost to be endured
in this forgetful distance.

My Grandfather's Funeral

I knew the dignity of the words:
"As for man, his days are as grass,
As a flower of the field so he flourisheth;
For the wind passeth, and he is gone"—
But I was not prepared for the beauty
Of the old people coming from the church,
Nor for the suddenness with which our slow
Procession came again in sight of the awakening
Land, as passing white houses, Negroes
In clothes the colors of the earth they plowed,
We turned, to see bushes and rusting roofs
Flicker past one way, the stretch of fields
Plowed gray or green with rye flow constant
On the other, away to unchanging pines
Hovering over parallel boles like
Dreams of clouds.

                At the cemetery the people
Surprised me again, walking across
The wave of winter-bleached grass and stones
Toward his grave; grotesques, yet perfect
In their pattern: Wainwright's round head,
His bad shoulder hunched and turning
That hand inward, Luby Paschal's scrubbed
Square face, lips ready to whistle to
A puppy, his wife's delicate ankles
Angling a foot out, Norwood Whitley
Unconsciously rubbing his blue jaw,
Locking his knees as if wearing boots;

The women's dark blue and brocaded black,
Brown stockings on decent legs supporting
Their infirm frames carefully over
The wintry grass that called them down,
Nell Overman moving against the horizon
With round hat and drawn-back shoulders—
Daring to come and show themselves
Above the land, to face the dying
Of William Henry Applewhite,
Whose name was on the central store
He owned no more, who was venerated,
Generous, a tyrant to his family
With his ally, the God of Moses and lightning
(With threat of thunderclouds rising in summer
White and ominous over level fields);
Who kept bright jars of mineral water
On his screened, appled backporch, who prayed
With white hair wispy in the moving air,
Who kept the old way in changing times,
Who killed himself plowing in his garden.
I seemed to see him there, above
The bleached grass in the new spring light,
Bowed to his handplow, bent-kneed, impassive,
Toiling in the sacrament of seasons.

II

Worse than the worst we had feared, they see,
Has come to pass. They tell us
To bother no longer with hope.
They have become in themselves
Parts of the great disgust.
Now they are closing down language
Into stones and toes. They sit
Each in his bleak cave
Darker than the boredom of a yawn. None
Will strike bone's sparks to a pitch heart.
It has become a block of pork.

The Sunplane

Upper Room rusts religiously into the Reader's Digest.
Jesus is praying, a light is about his countenance.
Catalogues of hardware promote lawnmowers and speedboats.
Sunlight circles with specks: yellow for these pages.
One whole cluttered story is devoted to the wreckage
Of childhood. Chemistry sets, ball bats, wasps' nests.
The thread of my labyrinth begins somewhere in there,
In the control-line model I never made fly or in the Cleveland
Kit of a Stinson Reliant which is still unbuilt.
Its plans are clear and full-sized, the scale exact,
The balsa twigs still yellow, crumbly, and light.
I could build its skeleton still as from a fist full of beams,
To rise on the tissue I now know how to shrink taut
Toward an early-morning sun. I'd have no hesitation
In leaving the house, dew I'd mark with my feet
Shows no single step back. The motor is turned
By solar batteries of silicon, the most powerful for their weight,
That I've ordered from *Edmund Scientific*. Steadily as sunlight
Rises, the Stinson rises, clearing the slender
Little trees edging in the ball diamond's outfield
(A small enough space to fly models in), leaving below
In the past one moody boy with a hand-launch glider,
As the Stinson rises reliant on wings of all things
I've labored to learn since then, and lay now in offering
Before those unsatisfied hours, my forehead brooding
In a bramble outfield, whose trees' names I couldn't untangle.

O Stinson I build you yet! Rise with the light.

Leaf Mirrors

Along a dustless clay road in wet weather,
    from the wide leaves there radiates
a presence of coolness and green, like water.

And the field of white weeds, delicate
    flattened umbrellas or mushroom heads;
Queen Anne's lace, so nearly flowers,

white sprays of unkempt blossom
    cocked in numberless angles to one another,
strung as if by invisible attraction

to the scattered clouds; and those soft-brushed
    billows seem deeply filamented,
potential with rain. Such

water-mirroring leaves ineffably unite
    with clouds in this light deepened by haze,
like trees regarding their figures in a pond.

The cloud-strung weeds, leaved clouds, shimmering
    holding a water-depth, connection
like consciousness, diminish

me shaped into the mosaic foliage,
    summer that is summer by passing; but mirror
my shared life between them, beyond me; suggest.

William Blackburn, Riding Westward

Here in this mild, Septembral December, you have died.
Leaves from the black oaks litter our campus walks,
Where students move, or stand and talk, not knowing
Your wisdom's stature, illiterate in the book of your face.

So often we walked along the old stone wall at night,
Looked up at your window, where lamplight cleft your brow,
And knew you were suffering for us the thornier passages,
Transfixed by *Lear*, or staring ahead to the heart
Of Conrad's Africa. Sometimes we ventured inside,
To be welcomed by an excellent whiskey, Mozart's *Requiem*.
This clarity of music and ice revealed once in air
A poem as you read it: as Vaughan created "The World,"
Eternity's ring shining "calm as it was bright."

On a wall was the picture of you riding on a donkey,
Caught in mid-pilgrimage, to a holy land I do not remember.
But your missionary parents had born you in Persia,
And after we'd learned that we saw you as explorer;
From hometowns scattered on an American map marked
Terra incognita for the heart, you led treks
Into our inward countries, and still seem discovering before,
Through straits to "the Pacific Sea," or the "Eastern riches."
Left on these New World shores—so thoroughly possessed,
So waiting to be known—on all sides round we see
Great trees felled and lying, their bodies disjointed,
Or standing in all weather, broken, invaded by decay.

The worn landscape of your features, the shadows
Days had cast under eyes, were part of the night

That steadily encroaches on the eastward globe, as it rotates
In sunlight. Out of your age shone a gleam of youth,
Which seems with cedars' searing to sing in the forest
In wolf's ears of green flame.
                                        Still, you are dead.
Your system is subject to entropy. Cells' change
Reduced your monarchical features to a kingship of chaos.
"With faltering speech, and visage incomposed,"
You said good night, between pangs of the withering hunger
Which filled your dying dreams with apples and cheeses.

In spite of the revolt of your closest ally, your body,
You died with the nobility you'd taught, and teaching, learned.
And now you roam my brain, King Lear after death.
The broken girl in your arms is only your spirit,
A poor fool hanged by Cordelia, by the straits of fever.

We visit your old office on campus in grief.
Outside, trees lift winterward branches toward
A sky in chaos. The patterning which spins the stars
Exists outside this weather we live under.

We see only branches against those clouds' inclemency.

III

Looking for a Home in the South

I

This particular spring day, March 19, 1973,
Is tearing at itself with insanities of traffic. Trucks
Of construction components, trucks of concrete, bulk like what
        is real.
I try to look through this particular day as through the doorframe
        of an abandoned house.
Squinting around the foreground, the shoulders of metal, I glimpse
Where apple tree boughs in wind strummed washboard
        clapboard.

II

Closer home, the tin on barns rusts as with a memory of mules.
A few houses cling, through camellias and columns, to an
        illusion,
Whose substance of grace never ruled within a South which
        existed.
But where is this land, which showed to our old ones as an
        horizon in the future.
And now, for us, is secret in the hovering of the past?

Was it a juice which awoke from grassroots snapped in plowing?
Even now the broken-top trees tap down into a soil below this
        moment.
The sap of it tightens around bulbs, squeezing up jonquils, wild
        onions.

III

Off the highway and almost there, tobacco barns and houses are
    bare to the sky.
A sparrow hawk has leaped from the light wire, leaving me
    balancing
In a wind that is chilled between hurt and delight.
My great grandfather's stone looks white from his iron-fenced
    graveyard
The color of briars, the fields that he keeps in his watch are
    combed with new furrows.

IV

This particular spring day, over which we are constructing
    despair
With materials of depression and concrete, the land we have
    missed, lying hidden,
Trickles and glistens in the dark, radiant to roots. Will none of us
Live to live into the unalloyed sunshine this land would learn to
    give us?

Discardings

Sometimes going back toward together I find
Me with lost, no-count, low-down and lonely:
Single with trees in logged-over evening,
Sun on us bound to go down.

Things lying low are sipped by the weather.
Black-strap creeks seem a slow molasses
Toward horizons thirsty with gravity.

Today in trees I kicked an old bucket
Full of woes, the chipped enamel like knotholes.
Burrows raised lids under leaves; quick fur
Eyes were on my face. Under the trash pile
I heard them like trickles of water,
Tunneling the sun down.

Home, when I pour bourbon and remember
A holed rubber boot on a hill of leaves,
It must be their sounds I am drinking.

I salute a boot from the foot
Of an unheralded cavalry. A black man
Walked furrows behind a mule whole years, unhorsed
By no war but the sun against the moon.

I drink branch water and bourbon
To the boards of his house that the wind
Has turned to its color and taken entirely.

Visit with Artina

She lives in a house whose color is bone left out
In the weather, over-lap siding gone pallid as wood ash.
A sheen condenses out of air on the polished grain.
Three little ones, their hair braided up in corn-rows,
Flock at her skirts, touch hands to her knees for comfort.
She is seventy, rake-handle thin, her shanks are bowed,
Her hip is troublesome ("some days I jes can't go");
Peculiar highlights luminesce on her cocoa skin.
Her hands are white inside, and shape whatever
She says in the air, or touch her three to be good.

"That ten dollars a week I used to get—I was study'en on it
Yesterday. I raised Joseph, Bernice, Wilma Doris, and theirs,
And they didn't never go hungry, we always had more
Than cornbread and greens 'a sett'en on the stove (lives
Of collard greens pile high in the room) I did it, Lord,
And now I feel good, jes like the little birds 'a sailing
In the air" (her fingers are bones for believable wings).

"Back when I worked for your folks—I felt burdened down,
Like everybody else was up higher." The right hand hovers
Over the left, in a different world. "For three years I dreamed
This dream, when I got down sick. It was all a dark cloud."
One palm wipes the air full of darkness over
The plastic flowers, the brown-earth sofa. "And a great crowd
Of people. They was troubled, trouble was among 'em.
I was to lead 'em, I was among 'em but I was apart.
I walked in the middle between 'em but I was far off."
Her hands have quarried cloud-pillars from the troubled air.
"An so I could get 'em there, he gave me a star."

One sure finger, in all the blue spaces of her room,
Picks out this point, maybe floating lint or a sungrain
Alone, places it, a star, in the middle of her forehead.
"An my mother, an my grandmother, what was Mothers in the
            church;
I 'scerned 'em on a hill, a way off." Her palms smooth the air.
She makes white robes with her palms. "I 'scerned 'em on a hill."

"These were the words that were give me: 'by the grace of God
I shall meet you.' " The house of her skin is strangely sheened,
Like sky-reflection polishing boards, or color
Rain water has caught from the air, in whatever low place.

Bordering Manuscript

I am alert to these letters in extraordinary numbers: perhaps
  from grass heavy-headed with seed, flickering a's and r's
under pressure of sun that I recognize as holy and intended—
  while a bird of indecipherable mind is scrolling margins of air.
A gold, illegible word rests on the left hand of vision.
  Illusions of its spelling leaf from the lacquer of hedges past
exits of buildings. Women removed across hundred-foot stretches
  of chained grass evoke vowels with their liftings of hair,
but let me confess: the name could be a man's as well as a
  woman's.
People printed with my children and wife in the foreground,
  though
accurate and clear, seem from a sufficient, forgetful distance
  to twine into the gigantic characters which fit no speech.
Places redolent with heat and resinous pines of meetings
  perhaps ten years ago form amber in retrospect.
The puzzle I see has thousands of pieces, each poor day
  hiding its two or one. Had I all the days permanently together,
I could assemble the jig-sawed chips in a lifetime. This thought
  chills me close to a water-like stillness, tea-colored and brackish
with vacations on rivers, as if a plane of focus shimmering behind
  the tear in a photograph, or body of air from all fields
inhabiting a music. Behind my lips, tipping my unknown
  tongue, she waits in her surface, her name my speech's mistress.

IV

To Alexander Solzhenitsyn, in Exile

Safe in the West, you will be watched over henceforth
By citizen press and police, officials elected
Through only our typical corruptions, administrators of hospitals
Where in your declining years these deeds will buy you
Easy entrance if then you are rich and remembered.

Our wire services distort your words, your bearded face,
Bleared from primitive terror in Russia the mother,
Is ironically represented by these crowding photographs.
Some will suspect, once you are tarnished by quick
Years of news, your noble treason not notable after all,
Since they have allowed you to live, it appears. But exile,
In your case, fits a capital offense. I imagine
Faulkner banished from the South he passionately confessed,
Whitman forbidden to walk the streets of his comrads'
                    Manhattan.
No, your crime was grave, and you have been desperately
                    punished.
Your treachery was true, and now you must wander your days
Past averted eyes in mirrors of newsprint, glimpsing
Burlesques of your face caged with the vended pages.

Henceforth you walk as a writer on the soil that is sealed
In your head, now you must be both roots and their landscape,
Oh may you wander a vast and fertile Russia of memory.
Another martyr's victory of conscience is won,
For you have forced them, fighting you, to lie openly again:
They have told you that your land is not your land.

A Kid at the County Fair

Cocoons tasted sweet on cones, potatoes fried,
Squeals squeezed out of girls as a Bomber dived.
Rita Moreno's lids made slits. Her offer
Boiled down to this: we'd eye her tits for a quarter.
A sign on a silver trailer by the spotlight's tongue
In the night told of a girl inside in an iron lung.
We gave to go in. She lay in a metal cylinder
Moved at the foot convulsively by a metal lever.
Face under shadow, she surrendered herself to a breath
That hissed. Outside, I sensed the arc-light spit
And erect its column, each particle electric, separate.
The motorcycle mounting centrifugally in the "Drum of Death"
Turned the fair in a vortex. I stepped to earth a recruit, intent
On a wound. Air moved coarse between my teeth,
Atoms of electricity and grease. I walked from the accident.

The Homeplace

I

The doorhandle odd and living in Arthur's hand
Was warm from the sunlight. Back from the hospital at Duke
In his Sunday suit blue as the shine of a stove flue,
He felt as if he couldn't get across the dust that was snaked
By old roots. The house looked over him with a two-story
        wisdom
From times before the Civil War, seeing in imperfectly
A head full of sun and air with its hand-blown panes.

The pick-up's seat was hot. When he drew in his breath,
Skin on the inside of his chest seemed delicate as cellophane.
Rays from a cone of cobalt had glowed his body clear through
Like sun on a new leaf.
                  Across the road out of town
Straight as the promise made to him by the owner of the farm,
Tobacco was growing, like a chest-high jungle half tamed,
Sullenly standing at attention, green as a rain forest.
He'd begged Mr. William just to let him finish his crop;
Now he didn't know if he was able. It seemed like he couldn't
Push out the front of his chest against the pressure of sunlight.
His bones hurt like they were threaded inside by silver wires.

He saw Mr. William's car coming directly from town.
He sat still in his truck till the dust had quit following
Its wheels. When he saw the bald head moving against the
        stubborn
Second story, where Mr. William's father had been born,
Some kind of call or will from the people who had mastered
These fields came down into his body and raised him to walk.

"How is it, Arthur? Did they say anything different this time?"
Mr. William's eyes roamed the fields, the swampward horizon,

Discovering shapes out of silence to answer his question.
"What the doctors say doesn't matter. Keep straight with me,
Keep hold of the drinking, and I promise the crop stays yours."
Dragging as if for life on a Lucky Strike,
Arthur turned back toward the house, which over his head
               watched
An old imperfection across the fields it held in mind.

II

August light, heavily bending elbow onto barn and sheds,
Glanced hard to the eye. Cropping had climbed up stalks
And twenty barns were in. In a leisure of dew that morning
He hardly believed, Arthur had taken his grandson fishing
At the swampside water. Tommy had landed a bass, there
Where dirt rimmed the drag-line pond like Confederate
               breastworks.

Arthur had a feeling past words for his struggle that season.
Nobody but him could know how he'd tried with a will
Beyond his own, though the trees called to him to sit still.
He felt like a soldier cut off somewhere, holding out
Against certain defeat, but going on for reasons the thinking
Of a man can't fathom: him being Mr. William's man
First because of money, later out of something more,
Serving in an infantry on a side he'd not chosen,
That chose him by bearing him there, alive into the sunlight.
But his breathing was better and he'd gained back weight,
Even if the silver pain still flashed through his bones.
He felt like maybe they would make it, he had the hands
In order, already today they were working the big field.

Now he walked through the military ranks of tobacco
And out toward the looping shed, to tell Joe Ellis
To get back there with the croppers and let Tommy rest.
It seemed like distances were changing, blacks in shadow
Were nearer then too far away, and his feet mired down
In soft hot new plowing like ridged-up ashes.

Crumpling the cellophane wrapper from a pack of Luckies,
Arthur lit one up and tried to walk on. His breath
Squeezed up under his throat and he remembered the second
When the bass's life had shone in its eye and then burst
Without changing except the clear film dulled and ebbed.
He choked back his breath, that was trying to get out,
And lifted his feet from miring in the furrows
Though the soil sank softer than quicksand and tripped him
Like creepers of a swamp, and he pitched to his knees, seeing
Dark boles of an old old forest ahead of him forever
On his hands and knees, but he knew that Mr. William
Would see the plowed field clear in the hard sunlight
So he struggled off his knees from in shade of trees that old
Must have been planted before the Civil War or some war before
And back into the sunlight, but couldn't see the shed or loopers,
Only knew himself full in view of house and windows
Poking head up over the faraway horizon like a cloud,
And emitted from his nostrils and mouth that bubble
Bright clear as the fish's last instant glance
That floated before and burst into the round of the sun:
A new dark shining that burned him with the opening of its
          circle.

When his feet came clear of a soil in shape of his body,
Arthur raised his eyes obediently to the wood-crossed windows,
Moved his knees obediently to march through the accumulated
Sunlight which had gathered in a shimmer into their panes,
Walked undefeated in a vision which had witnessed his death
When he was born, held for him now his upstairs bed like deep
water.

Revisitings

The sky is low and close and light is a mist.
Sunday makes shine a still more sultry water
In this summer air. Grass returns prodigal with seed.
These birds that perk and skip seem living souls.
Magnolia flowers are reminiscent of childhood and candles.
Past a line inscribed on leaves by a bobwhite's whistle,
I suspect a different self like a nobler brother.
Mimosa trees in flower, piles of clouds
In an horizon without perspective, help me recall.
I sit on the hill of an avenue of trees, feeling
That I want to say hush, hush, to the traffic.
For a little while I feel close again to a person
Who one time existed under immensely tall trees.
A wind from where shadows are generating rain tells me
This day stands always in pools behind doors I have closed.
How have I closed away my best self and all of his memories?
Many of the tongues of grass are speaking to the sun,
Obscured for a moment, in a language of vapor from underneath.

V

Zeppelin Fantasy

I fly on the Hindenburg, though last night
My dreams were of flame. Inside the sound
Of motors is an aluminum piano. Its icy
Tones bare teeth of diamond, whose grin
Chills the bosom of an American heiress.
Languages are eaten with a salad of medals
By the satin stripes of trousers. Girders
Elliptical as sleep invent our night
Above the Atlantic. We dance in a dream
Like a politician's black cigar.

War Summer

In our tin-roofed house in the big war's summer,
In a somnolent town in sunlight's dominion,
I read of the Shalott of Lord Tennyson,
Dreaming beyond guardrooms of the distant thunder
To a city in that sun's blind center.

How odd in my upstairs room, awake
In attic air, in wrath of the sun,
Except for my balsa Spitfire, alone,
Unable to descend, where my father'd mistake
My desire as he massed his jaws at steak.

Would that ardor of sunflame never relent?
My thoughts were a web as in the Lady's tower.
Tinkering tissue and sticks toward the power
Of flight, I dreamed all communion as ascent.
Our rapport in combat came only at twilight.

Through rumble of distant thunder, far
Flash of the six o'clock news. Under each
Portentous cloud, we turned from our workbench
Stunned. Radio's tone warned static; came roar
Above houses, artillery of a wide atmosphere.

Cartographers

Chief of Air Staff Portal, Sir Arthur Harris
For bombers—this brokerage in apocalypse—are men
In the dark. All that they've asked has been given:
Aircrews, Merlins, "Window," the Tallboy bomb.
Harris alone has visceral purpose: to eliminate
Germany's cities in gradual stages.
                       Theory, perhaps,
Is at fault. The aims of Strategic Bombing attained,
The planes cannot sight, through mists of a new year's weather,
Upon the last of "Morale." A further demonstration,
An "Operation Thunderclap," will deliver the effect of Last Day,
Signal a nation of the imminence of Judgement.
The Americans' Spaatz and Marshall, Sinclair, Minister
For Air, Churchill himself, share in complicity.
They require some city of the East, one swollen as of old
With travellers. *Leipzig, Dresden, Chemnitz.* Old names
Promiscuously bandied about. These, after all, are delivered
By events into their hands. In January of the war's
Last year, God, if he exists, is very weak.

Your sons and daughters of the Hun, sleep fitfully.
A pencil is passing you over, marked city by city.
Its touch on a map is Destiny. Spaatz is seduced
From "precision." Harris of Bomber Command distrusts
The "panacea target," where something is aimed at
Other than the whole of your lives. "Shall we forsake
This most substantial substance for a most tenuous shadow?"

These words by Harris. Ball bearings, oil, not substance
Enough for his bombers. One city is circled from the map
His enemy. Even cities are losing substance in his hands.
He has them all in his hands. He models, of frangible
Dresden, a final event. Cartographer of fire.

At Raleigh Memorial Gardens

(Post Christian Era)

A Jesus in marble watched over trees for miles
(Their consciences cloud). From the level
Of a basketball rim, he looked benign like a machine.
I witnessed the distant antennas.
Sunlight rippled flowers in urns, parturition
Of a minnow of a jet from the airport horizon.
By a pond with lilies,
A mother and her three children
Were walking alive.
My footsteps shuddered to grass, to clay
With ice quartz bits, to a slope below which the pond
Shivered in involuntary ripples.
The dead were rocking lightly in their coffins.
The eyes of a flock of fingerling fish nudged at my hands,
Were showed no bread. "You are not my flock," I spoke.
An elastic stretched out of my chest
Clearer than quartz, taut in threads between
Those eyes of Jesus, a woman's hair, antennas
In Titan-march to dimensions of pins punctuating a horizon.

VI

Eden's Dinosaur

I

Where Wilson stays "niggertown" from childhood,
Walled in like a cemetery with stone, one yard keeps
This concrete dinosaur. Shadows cast by bamboo,
Oriental otherworldly stripes of dark and light, surround
Recollection. Through an inverted arch, hard objects exist:
Concrete bird bath, boulder by a pool, table and benches.
Unexpected plants inhabit the background
Of a circle of wall I'd never stepped through
Into the garden of an Alice I imagine as in a negative.

Closed in by waking, in the worthless, advertised present,
How would I pass that gate? Perhaps I'd wade memories
To the door, send a chime sounding into underwater rooms.

II

It summoned the maker's daughter, brought up through fossilized
Times like many summers' shade his name preserved
As by ice or salt within these walls of original granite.
His picture was on the mantle: bearded, "ahead of his time," as
          she put it.
He'd returned, an architect, from Tuskegee, to build this ark of
          a house,
Create its animals, keep close by his side a favorite daughter,
Whose lips kept the story of a walk's mosaic:
"Here baby, hand me that color," or some other, she remembered,
In words out of the walled yard inviolate around her childhood.
Her marriage in New Jersey was a dream, this the rock house she
          returned to.
I see his artistry in the rooms, his almost feminine spirit:

A semicircular table with crochet, completed by an arching
        window.
I felt how he had walled them in with stones of his love
Into a yard complete with fish pond and miniature furniture,
About a well whose water at one time would frost your glass.

III

Now of the animals, only the dinosaur,
Its child whose arc of a tail is broken, remain
In this world. His comic strip snout
Seems no longer dumb:

                         I am evolution's ghost,
I am things let die with brain unfinished.
I have a share-cropper face and flattened-off paws
Disinherited by his dexterous hands.
What was his purpose as he fathered me? I make
A sad kind of monument, an uprearing animal
Instead of the statue of a soldier or a marble angel.
He looked into my eyes this unending finality
That day his heart failed him in a tree, pruning for a neighbor—
Upreaching still—him, with his beard and brain, the very image of
        a maker.

Whose yard and wall now resemble a cemetery's slow thought.

The Man

Screened porches, white churches, declined into
Cemeteries with Rodin's *Hands in Prayer*
Cast of cement. Laciness of pecans over
Flat-country houses, expanding the sky,
Relaxed their holds on cornfields. There grew
Rows of receivers on poles, refreshment
Bars with rest rooms, screens with flesh-toned
Kisses giant against twilight: movies
X-ed to damnation among steeples of sermons.
The land dreamed in color of old summer,
Heard long-drawn mourning dove's distresses
Consoling with sadness. Rivers turned over
In slumber, oil-slick ripples boiling up
From thought's turmoil underneath. Ravines
Shaped tissue of day into swathes over highways,
Where elastic air that snaps after lightning
Heals into silence behind the ripping of motors.
Rock out-crops, gravel fire-tower trails
Still slumbered their deer and foxes, pranked
Opossums into garbage and night streets of cities.

What the red clay flanks can't form is their Adam
Under incubating sunlight, spinning dust
Devils as they must, in blasphemies of the man.

Water tank towers are lonesome, mechanical,
Their striding illusory in a rear-view mirror.
Twenty-foot Jesus spreads his arms in vain
In white cement for the vaulted dead.
T. V. towers spidery with wires speak

Electromagnetic waves indecipherable
As Etruscan. Sunlight showers its gold,
A mythological spotlight, empty. Its hero
Must sculpt on air, his head and hand
Huge beneath a cumulus, shapes which answer
Our ancient nostalgia for the city of the sun's
White springing. He must geometrize
And simplify the sentiment of our hearts
With a hard art pointed as fire.

Before messages were lost into media
This man's aquiline features countenanced
The shapes of Chichén Itzá. He moves
Beyond electrical contrivances, tensioning
Horizons, desires his towers, would metal
Cruciform gods from these carriers of wires.

A Southern Elegy

April, 1974

I

To picture the authentic locality of Lee's reputation:

Was it corn-stubble cabins, columns bemused by the ridges
In mindless Tennessee? Along the snake-winding mahoganies
Of the Chickasaw, the Pee Dee, the Chickahominy, the Haw, the
    Susquehanna?

Moss in beards, arthritic knees of cypresses, would have soughed
Of the fitness of his courses without a motion of breath.
Bass-fat lakes, scummed over with gore of sunsets,
Would ruminate victory through evenings loaded with thunder.

Parisian silhouettes in the ballrooms of Richmond,
Locomotives' funnels on Petersburg sidings,
Were by themselves insufficient to hew out a polished space

From swampland oblivion, whose elegists were only mosquitoes.
The wonder is that names emerged at all
From such quicksand states and counties of woodland,
With such unthinkable horseback miles to cover:
Sloughs into which Hannibal and all his elephants might fall.

II

The voice of FDR, grave with Pearl Harbor,
Echoed along hallways of radio to threatened California.
What electricity of rumor overarched horizons
When Lee bestrode Traveller at Gettysburg?

Our minds are suspended from beacon to guyed beacon
In words across the sunsets, Sherman in diesel rigs
Rumbles this present day to our sea, Atlantas
Of pine trees fall to the chain saw's ricochet.

III

A stage expands above farms, electrons' phosphor
Over trees and streams, the gatherers of earliest mists,
Above crests still swollen with breastworks.
Towering names remain, casting like shadows
The absences of figures: misguided McClellan, A. P. Hill,
Sheridan and Stuart with cavalry toward Richmond.
Forrest, Longstreet, Pickett of Cemetery Ridge.

A stony Grant rigidly on horseback, photographed, faces
The stovepipe height of Lincoln in rumple-leg dignity:
One figure equal in dimension to his legitimate theater.

The luminous eye of Lee is gone, with jaw-line of honor
And resolve. Fanatical intensity of Jackson is missing.

Lee. Lincoln. As Nixon jowls our land's automatic eye.

Visiting Chancellorsville

While the western sky is paling from violet to lilac
I approach the Confederate cannon on Hazel Grove.
Union gun pits at Fairview seem still their aim.
How well the earth remembers! Ground is ridged
In the still trees like one long burial furrow,
A wave of soil cresting steadily toward a different shore.
One musket's arc past the highway, Stonewall Jackson
Fell wounded. The overpowering supply of the Union
Rumbles on along concrete lanes. I am haunted by Jackson's
Expression in a photograph, by the reconstructed house where he
            died,
Of pneumonia, in presence of his wife, with amputated arm.
Hill-crest cedars grow perfect in a levelling rose.
For this place, the movement of times is finished.
The scalloped gun pits, which grass has sealed to the rain,
Hold only the air of a day which created them by battle.
Broom sedge slopes between cannon take the hue of breath
From sunset. Only this keeps permanent:
These cedars, these gun pits, these breathless.

VII

Gift of Inheritance:
A Sequence

The Capsized Boat

I

My father was launching his speedboat
Through vines by the bridge.
Dark bottomed clouds were walking the sky.
Wet air enfolded like cloth, looked
Glassy in light between trees. Mosquitoes
Drenched in the leaf-smell
Tangled like creepers. Hard cold drops
From a shade that moved higher than trees' shade
Had spattered the stream.

II

After the shower I jumped for the cockpit.
The stern wave of another speedboat challenged our passing.
We crowded the creek with our thunder
All the way from Ruffin's Bridge. Father crouched before
The Evinrude motor. He drove by his desire
Our red prow across the slant wave.
I faced deep into a clammy sigh of water, which clung
Across the light and went cold.
Father pulled me alive from that odor of dying,
Swam up under the capsized boat
And saved me to my name. His overalls
Heavy with money, he hauled me into light of his example.

Lawn and Light

His mower whirred cut grass like dust
Through daylight gray as if seen through windowscreen, spun
Raw cut scent of wiregrass into the dusk.
His short muscular figure strained erect
While I was prostrate on the sideporch couch with fever,
But I knew from intensely seeing
The light raining gray over his stiff effort
Bringing the night with lawnmower sleepier than crickets
That he was becoming a part of me forever.

I knew even then the sadness of a memory
To be, even as the shape of his strength
And turn of his mower, sweet
Like the strained music of a summer fan,
Held me from dying.

On the Homefront

I

Plate glass gazed on the depot. Auto parts wholesale.
Air brakes' coughs in switchyards, odor of metal.
A vacuum draws me: the wake of my father's words.

Nothing would be well said or ill, for order was by number:
So little part for me to play, I seem not present
In the memory.
           Down the known aisles shelved to their ceilings,
We'd break upon a cave of mechanics, who bent in surrounding
Some motorblock open like a sacrificed carcass: hapless,
Greased. Plates and containers were set everywhere.
Unpalatable fluids. The point of the calendars were pictures,
Pin-up poses, nipples like the fuses of shells
Or nacelles of aircraft. An *artist's conception*. She reflected
Blessings onto hoods from the enameled tones of her limbs.

II

Preparation of a meal of oil. Everyone
Wiping his hands with mill waste, secretly pleased.
She on the calendar curved sleeker than metal.
The sizes of bolts were language.
These pale inner-temple mechanics, during daylight,
Practiced the refinement of cylinder and piston.

A Vigil

I

Thanksgiving sacrament, piety of crystal and silver.
Platters and dishes passed on from hand to hand.
Words so well-worn they drone with the summertime fan.
My grandfather blessing, his countenance fields in the sunlight.

I waited beside him for words, for what he'd gathered
From hawks wheeling sun, oak leaves' tension under glare.
He rocked in the parlor with a bible, his face grown taciturn,
The hooked nose indian, hair as if filamented down.
His parchment skin was the season's hieroglyphic.
Going for water, I passed through the company parlor:
Mantle with mirror and clock, stiff plush and varnish.

II

One window overlooked the trees of the creek, where silt
From high water on leaves seemed dust from the passing days.

I poured from a pitcher. Tracing a beaded trickle,
Sweat down a frosted tumbler. Sensation of October
In August. I thirsted to bring into potable solution
These motes of dust that swam the green shade's sunbeam.
I sat on the porch beside him, spell-bound by columns.
Horizon woven to softening by orbits of swallows.

"It's been eighty-six years and it seems like a day."

A Garden's Season

I

Divided from it now by this distance, I see our garden
Beyond or between these simple things which cannot define it.
Air outdoors and for children but crossed by gleams
From the Thanksgiving silver. Within a high board fence, where
      grandmother's
Roses were bordered with bricks, we played in the dirt.

The place of our dream remains tangent, though I recall
Also a concrete fish pond, a tree beside it
Either always in blossom or with cherries showing perfect as
      marbles.

Gold fish hung from the surface like impressions of flame,
Whatever shadows passed over of a little girl and boy:
First selves I see as in an Easter-time photograph.

With fronded hair like the hyacinths, she dressed in velvet.
Like fish in those tones of silver and a rose, we swam
In the high wall's shadow, its atmosphere our drink and shelter,
Food to our mouths with Thanksgiving crystal and cherries.

II

Its trunk grown thick with our grandfather's years, the pecan
Waved leaves above like the upstairs rooms high as clouds;
Dried sage and furniture, bottles, frames to stretch curtains,
Would wait for us there until we'd ever have need of them,
Probably forever. Clouds moved over like wind across a pond,
Printing our faces and bodies with foliage they rippled.

Iron River

I was taken to a cousin's on the Pamlico river. Through old trees
I looked along moldering streets to the riverfront sunk
Below sunlight. Hulks wallowed mud among the weeds.
Sidewalks stank to my thoughts with imminent water.

I settled exiled upstairs in a house held hostage
On its lower story by swirl and brown eddy; stuffed feathers
I picked from my pillow into an emptied cold cream jar,
To be tossed like a castaway's bottle from this tower window.
I bunched soap bubbles in a bowl like grapes, straw stem
Joining them still to my breath, so that rainbow membranes
Jointed like a lung would move with my chest.
                                                    Later,
A vacation house of the Brooms', bare rooms, eyed pine.
Drumming of the tugs at night re-echoed like war.
Mazie and Aunt Elsie talked, while pines brushed the screens,
In an unfamiliar pungence of tone, of Haywood, Haywood
          Broom.
This man's complexion sounded the color of broom sedge, his
          breathing
A rustle. Broom, Broom, with the night's cannonading
Of tugs, Haywood and his lungs, deadly *sanitorium.*

With Darkening Foliage

Recovering from rheumatic fever, I lay on our side porch couch,
An uncle to read to me. Tobruk, Rommel, Montgomery, El
    Alamein.
I was as pleased with the North Africa campaign as with our lawn
Attracting the evenfall and dew with level-cut tuft,
Releasing soaked-in light in lightning bugs' effervescence.
I hung on his words by the bulb as they lanterned into our old
    pecan
Topheavy with darkening foliage. I remember a desert soldier
As equipped in *Mechanix Illustrated*: his pack his boots his
    Thompson gun,
These articles of invulnerable mastery. Remember now the
    photographs
Sensationalizing thought: the twin-boom P-38 test-firing
At night, tracers of its machine guns and cannon a fiery sword.
I suffered no doubt of these heroes' nature. They were Americans,
Righteous, and were brave. Night winds lashing the pecan
Past my window, explosions of summer storms' lightning,
Were atmospheres no more sweeping in tone than their anger and
    power.

Diamond of Shadow

It is the gray quiet fall of evening.
Dew is on the ball diamond stubble. We are
Bound for trees only more humped and shaped
To be hill-top still than the clouds,
Past the encircling outfield, over our knees in grass-shadow.
I have taken the next step and have fallen from my name,
Am behind or outside our occasion,
An odd thought only, absorbed in strangeness.

Expanding from that point and that moment,
I felt a radiant separation, sight without eyes
Over my own body's shoulder: me lost
In my footsteps, remembering as another.

A Forge of Words

I

Moths crowded streetlights revival evenings. The teenaged
Lingered long outside, reluctantly gathered.
The first hymn calling to sinners, bitter-mellow and lonesome,
Would detach us one by one from circumferences of light:
Circumscribed with shadow by a brim of tin, through leaves
Minnow-live in the wind. Still free among moths, we scraped
The wet sidewalk with reluctant soles, our shoulders flickered
                    over
By magnified wings, like fluttering shapes of our sins.

At last to resist no longer we moved up concrete
Steps, abandoning the afternoon's rain in our thoughts,
To chastize our gesture, flip away bravado like cigarettes.

II

To gather up later. Now to fit sensibly in a pew.
I see my thighs muscled wide in the trousers.
The reverend's eyesockets hollow under eventime lighting.
We weight his voice with our responses; as we bend in singing
We empower his beseeching.
                    Kneeling in shame at the altar,
I sense on the back of my neck that repentance is for women.
I turn and encounter the resolve in masculine faces.
Bill Tyson's leather folds and slab-flat cheeks
From his road-building weather. John Grimsley an ashed-over
            coal,
His face to front the seasons of farming unabashed
By salvation. My own father's jaws locked tight on the names
Of his sins, hardly bowed on his wrestler's neck;
This company of Christians grim like underworld gods.

From the anvil of Christ, I receive my hammered name.

Combat Station

Ralph with the corded triceps, with cleft chest wired
With black hair, told Marine Corps war. I wielded the spanner.
Our lift in the open sun made all metal stinging
In heat-thin oil. His talk was Australian women,
Severed American heads on a path in New Guinea.
The lens of an August atmosphere focused our labor.
Beads of tractors' rims were loosened with wedges.
We greased trailers and pick-ups, washed clay rivers
From rusted fenders in the waning afternoons.
At his headquarters desk where a cash register rang,
My father gave orders to receive the new assaults of customers.
We fought against being overrun, held wave after wave,
Fired slugs into chassis from the automatic greasegun,
My brother riddling fenders with a high-pressure hose.
No matter how we mauled at wedges, levered with tire tools,
Tugged at exhaust pipes blazing like machine guns,
Our general denied us victory by selling to the enemy.
Like heroes we fought for a stalemate, held out for sundown.
Staring into hubcaps, I remembered the metal of a P-47
That had cut through a grove of pines and broken in a field,
Pilot's blood jellied in the cockpit. My father's silhouette
Tightened the close-ringed horizon of trees, as I fought on
For the moment we could signal a roof above the gas pumps
To blaze up its pantheon of bulbs into creek-water evening,
When field moths would orbit their wattage like foliage in
       motion.

To Forgive this Inheritance

I

Sundays I pushed through hedges, crossed ditches by fields.
In a water-shimmer atmosphere of heat, a clapboard church
Gleamed its steeple white as Lot's salt wife.
I was not my father, not like him, I knew an intenser
Prayer than his. I had whispered it Saturday night
In my hard-won car on a dirt road that ran past trees.
Dark had been the cocoon for our tentative stirrings,
Air an elastic velvet scented with corn;
Moths over fields bore us up on their cumulative wings.

II

Sun wedged pincers of light through the bases of clouds.
My grandfather had stood in his pew and prayed for rain,
Asking a blessing on farmers dressed by the weather.

I passed cornblades on ridges curled dryly to tubes.
My vision through the clear air distilled its water,
A few drops thudded, spent bullets, into the soil.
I felt the sky's blue curve alive like a skin,
Turned toward creek and the rich thrusts of trees.
Overcast gathering in swirls had moistened the sun.
A few drops circled the mahogany polish of the stream.

My eye, through answered prayer, grasped the lean fish
Under images of cloud upon water stable as stones.

Images, Burning

I

I stumbled from the university library, blind with images
Of the Messerschmitt. The frail dissertation refused to progress.
Fantasies of war, actual as iron, obstructed
My notebooks. The learned doctors inhabited crumbling
Centuries, towers which toppled into the Battle of Britain.
Sunlight lay with a tigerish gleam on the innocent grass.

II

Reading of war, one must imagine the casualties:
Brave men trapped by canopies in airplanes on fire.
The Spitfires, the Messerschmitts, spin toward the sunlit sea
Or land below like leaves from the tree of man.
Imagination expands in gratitude to fact
That each white down must parachute its seed,
Dark kernel living or not, back into a green map.

The Dragon's Teeth

Tuned by contemplation, I crest a hill road
In the Uwharrie forest, first see bloom the flame
Which had plumed before my climb in a dark-tree cloud.
I join a young ranger watching to hold the fire
Between a ravine to the right of us and this nook of our road.
As wind swells changing he runs to unreel hose
Toward a new blaze to our left and I lope downslope toward
Dragonteeth men, marching as if springing out of earth,
Which the sparks have sewed. As I stamp upon
Half-black broomsedge and leaves lavender-rimmed with ignition,
The magical element tonguing my trousers my boots
Is orange on this overcast day.
It is only by my sidewise sweeping kicks of dirt
And rocks that these blazes are stayed. With an odor of burning
On boots and shirt and the drying of fresh sweat upon me,
Water is sweet from a canteen. I stand by the ranger
While he speaks of the certainty of arson. Farmers drive past
In pick-ups, pig fat forearms hooked over windowledge.
I watch him calculating which one must have set it.
I am happy to stand for a time by a professional manager
Of the dragontooth element, stand for a few more words
Before walking up a ridge which overlooks the Uwharrie hills
Like a snake's folds rising out of water.
I sit upon a rock to the harping of the winds of thought
Till it is a very long way to the back of my neck
And I feel beyond my shoulders voices moving silently as
           daylight.

Infant Hero

What if Christ is a name
For the heroic infant soul
Which awakens to itself one evening
On a hillslope passage,
Below trees that are real?

Mary and Joseph his parents,
Who took the babe,
Wrapped him in swaddling clothes
And laid him in a manger.

Laid him in rags and straw,
Held gifts to the wondering infant
(Frankincense and myrrh of the senses),

His clear white limbs as if folded petals
Or a knot carved in ivory.
To awaken only gradually to his name.

O flame
Ability to know
Sweet hurtless fragrance

First seeing swaddled in light:
Gold behind holy eyes
Of this family
Which shines in each aureole.

I scrub till the square of an old iron fence
Begins to come clear. Rust-eaten railing
Like a flaking cinder. I sweep out briars,
Am delicate about cutting the young trees.

Star-winking tangle of the slick briar leaves.
Sunlight timeless as creation. Birds
And dew and their voices sweeter than droplets
On each day dawning the beginning.

My great great grandfather's shaft is tilting awry
And clasped by vines. I break the dry tendril.

Candle of stone. Its flame
On top the years of sun.

Henry Applewhite
Born October 3, 1801
Died November 29, 1849
Orphia wife of Henry Applewhite
Born October 21, 1806
Died August 11, 1896
Our mother and father are gone but not forgotten.

Stone condensed from a history of weather.

I place three heads of wheat from the field
Outside on the gravestone of each. Mourning doves
And bobwhites are calling; a sprinkling
Like early raindrops at the edges of cloud.

A native of North Carolina, James Applewhite was reared in Stantonsburg in the tobacco-growing eastern part of the state. He spent several years studying informally with Randall Jarrell while in the department of English at the University of North Carolina at Greensboro. He has taught at George Washington University in Washington, D.C., and is currently associate professor of English at Duke University. Mr. Applewhite has received a Danforth Fellowship for excellence in teaching, an award from the National Endowment for the Arts for one of his poems, and at present he holds a Creative Writing Fellowship from the National Endowment for the Arts.